COMPLETE GUIDE TO DUCK FARMING

I0466559

Expert Techniques, Sustainable Practices, And Profitable Strategies For Raising Healthy Animals

GIOVANNI MALAKAI

DISCLAIMER

This book's content is solely intended for informational and educational purposes. The author and publisher of this book make no express or implied representations or warranties of any kind regarding the completeness, accuracy, reliability, suitability, or availability of the information, products, services, or related graphics contained in it, even though every effort has been made to ensure their accuracy and dependability. You consequently absolutely assume all risk associated with any reliance you may have on such material.

The author's own experiences and studies serve as the foundation for the techniques and procedures covered in this book. They might not be appropriate for every circumstance or person. Before putting any advice or recommendations from this book into practice, readers should use their own discretion and take into account their unique situation. Consulting with qualified professionals who specialize in veterinary care and

TABLE OF CONTENTS

CHAPTER ONE 13

INTRODUCTION TO DUCK FARMING.................................13

DUCK FARMING'S EVOLUTION AND HISTORY 13

BREEDS OF DUCKS...15

ADVANTAGES OF RAISING DUCKS....................................16

OBSTACLES IN DUCK FARMING 17

IMPORTANT WORDS AND DEFINITIONS 19

CHAPTER TWO 21

PUTTING YOUR DUCK FARM IN ORDER.............................21

CHOOSING AN APPROPRIATE LOCATION 21

CREATING AND BUILDING DUCK HOUSES..........................22

ESSENTIAL INSTRUMENTS AND EQUIPMENT 24

GETTING WELL DUCKLINGS 25

SETTING APART MONEY FOR STARTUP EXPENSES..............27

CHAPTER THREE 29

DIETARY AND FEEDING 29

THE NUTRITIOUS NEEDS OF DUCKS 29

FEED AND SUPPLEMENT TYPES.......................................30

FEEDING PLANS AND TIMETABLES...................................31

CONTROLLING THE QUALITY AND AVAILABILITY OF WATER 32

SPECIAL DIETARY REQUIREMENTS AND MODIFICATIONS 33

CHAPTER FOUR 35

MANAGEMENT OF HEALTH AND DISEASE 35

TYPICAL DUCK ILLNESSES AND HOW TO PREVENT THEM..................35

IMMUNIZATIONS AND HEALTH CARE 36

IDENTIFYING SYMPTOMS OF ILLNESS 37

PROCEDURES FOR QUARANTINING NEW BIRDS...........38

TIPS FOR MAINTAINING A HEALTHY FLOCK 39

CHAPTER FIVE..41

INCUBATION AND BREEDING..41

CHOOSING BREEDING STOCK...41

BREEDING METHODS AND RECOMMENDED PRACTICES 42

EQUIPMENT AND THE INCUBATION PROCESS 43

HANDLING DUCKLINGS AFTER HATCHING 44

MAINTAINING DOCUMENTS FOR BREEDING PROGRAMS 46

CHAPTER SIX..47

ENVIRONMENTAL MANAGEMENT AND HOUSING 47

CREATING COZY DUCK HOUSING 47

CONTROLLING DENSITY AND SPACE 48

CONTROLLING TEMPERATURE AND VENTILATION 49

BEDDING AND HANDLING OF LITTER 50

STRATEGIES TO PROTECT AGAINST PREDATORS 51

CHAPTER SEVEN 53

EVERYDAY HANDLING AND ADMINISTRATION 53

TYPICAL MAINTENANCE AND CARE 53

HOW TO MOVE AND HANDLE DUCKS SAFELY...................54

TRACKING THE HEALTH AND BEHAVIOR OF DUCKS..........56

ADJUSTMENTS FOR SEASONAL CARE................................57

EFFECTIVE TECHNIQUES FOR FARM MANAGEMENT 59

CHAPTER EIGHT 61

  SALES AND MARKETING 61

    FINDING OPPORTUNITIES IN THE MARKET 61

    FORMULATING A MARKETING STRATEGY AND BRAND 62

    PRICING METHODS FOR PRODUCTS AND DUCKS 63

    TRADER OF DUCKS AND DUCK PRODUCTS...........................64

    DEVELOPING RELATIONSHIPS WITH CUSTOMERS 66

CHAPTER NINE 69

  MONEY HANDLING...69

    FINANCIAL PLANNING AND BUDGETING 69

    STRATEGIES FOR COST MANAGEMENT AND REDUCTION 70

    MAINTAINING DOCUMENTS AND FINANCIAL MONITORING............71

    INVESTMENT AND FINANCING OPTIONS 73

    ANALYSIS AND STRATEGIES OF PROFITABILITY 74

CHAPTER TEN 75

  FAQS & FREQUENTLY ASKED QUESTIONS 75

    TAKING CARE OF COMMON ISSUES IN DUCK FARMING 75

    COMMONLY ASKED QUESTIONS 76

    TROUBLESHOOTING TYPICAL ISSUES 78

    SOURCES FOR ADDITIONAL EDUCATION 79

    SUGGESTIONS FOR PROLONGED ACHIEVEMENT...........................81

ABOUT THE BOOK

The "Complete Guide to Duck Farming" is a vital tool for those hoping to pursue a fulfilling career in duck farming. This in-depth book explores the origins and development of duck farming, providing readers with a profound comprehension of the practice's historical development. It helps farmers select the best breeds for their particular needs by offering comprehensive information on the many varieties of duck breeds. The book outlines the many advantages of duck farming, including the advantages it has for the environment and the production of meat and eggs. To make sure that readers are ready for the realities of this endeavor, it also discusses the difficulties encountered by duck farmers. The purpose of this is to acquaint readers with the key phrases and definitions related to duck farming.

Establishing a duck farm is an essential first step, and this guide provides professional guidance on where to put one as well as how to design and build duck housing.

It includes all of the tools and equipment needed to make sure everything runs smoothly. To lay a strong foundation for their farming business, readers will discover where to find healthy ducklings and how much money to set aside for initial expenses.

Nutrition and feeding are crucial to sustaining a healthy duck colony. The book covers several kinds of feed and additives as well as the dietary needs of ducks. It provides helpful guidance on controlling water availability and quality, as well as feeding schedules and routines.

Special nutritional needs and adaptations are also covered, ensuring that farmers can respond to the unique needs of their ducks.

Duck farming places a high value on managing health and disease, and this guide offers detailed information on common duck diseases and preventative measures. It goes on immunization and medical care, identifying symptoms of sickness, and new bird quarantine protocols.

There are also tips for keeping a healthy flock, which will assist farmers in keeping their ducks in the best possible shape.

Growing a duck farming enterprise requires successful breeding and incubation. The book contains breeding procedures and best practices along with advice on choosing breeding stock. It covers the procedure and tools needed for incubation as well as the post-hatching care of ducklings. Additionally included is record-keeping for breeding projects, which helps farmers monitor and enhance their breeding endeavors.

Duck farming requires careful attention to environmental management and efficient housing. This guide explains how to plan cozy duck housing while controlling density and space. It addresses managing bedding and litter, controlling ventilation and temperature, and predator safety techniques.

A duck farm needs daily management and attention to operate well. The book offers helpful guidance on normal upkeep and care, safe handling and transportation of ducks, and behavior and health monitoring. It also provides advice on how to manage farms more effectively and make adaptations for the changing seasons.

Sales and marketing are essential to a successful duck farming enterprise. Farmers can use the guidance to build a brand and marketing strategy, as well as to find market prospects. It covers selling ducks and their products, developing relationships with customers, and pricing methods for ducks and duck items.

A duck farming business needs sound financial management to remain viable. This book discusses financial planning and budgeting, record-keeping and financial tracking, and cost management and reduction techniques. Along with techniques to guarantee long-term success and profitability assessments, it also covers finance and investment choices.

The book includes a thorough FAQ section and answers frequently asked questions about duck farming. It makes sure readers have access to the knowledge they need to succeed by providing resources for additional learning as well as troubleshooting advice for typical issues. The handbook is a priceless tool for both new and seasoned duck farmers since it offers advice for long-term success.

CHAPTER ONE

INTRODUCTION TO DUCK FARMING

DUCK FARMING'S EVOLUTION AND HISTORY

The history of duck farming is extensive and goes back thousands of years. Ducks were first domesticated in Southeast Asia when native populations tamed wild ducks for their meat, eggs, and feathers.

These customs eventually extended to other regions of the world, which resulted in the creation of diverse duck breeds appropriate for varied environments and uses. According to historical accounts from ancient China and Egypt, ducks played a crucial role in agricultural life by facilitating trade and subsistence.

The techniques used in duck farming changed along with agriculture. Significant advances were made throughout the Industrial Revolution, including the introduction of specialized diets and better breeding techniques that increased growth rates and output.

Commercial duck farming grew in popularity in the 20th century, especially in North America and Europe where advances in science and technology allowed for even better breeding, nutrition, and disease prevention. During this time, intensive farming systems came into being, increasing productivity and production efficiency.

Duck farming is still evolving today thanks to sustainable practices and new technologies. Due to increased awareness of the effects on the environment and the welfare of animals, farmers are adopting more ethical and ecologically friendly farming practices. Modern innovations like climate-controlled housing, computerized feeding systems, and sophisticated health monitoring have made duck farming a highly productive and sustainable sector.

The cultural legacy and historical value of duck farming are preserved in many areas by the continued use of traditional practices despite these improvements.

BREEDS OF DUCKS

Duck breeds are varied and have distinct qualities that make them ideal for various farming applications. The Pekin, Muscovy, Khaki Campbell, and Indian Runner are among the most popular breeds. Chinese pekin ducks are a mainstay of commercial meat production because of their great meat quality and quick growth. They are easily managed because of their placid attitude, white feathers, and orange beak.

Originating in South America, Muscovy ducks are recognizable by their size and characteristic red-faced caruncles. They are perfect for organic and free-range farming since, in contrast to other ducks, they are comparatively quiet and have higher disease resistance. English-bred Khaki Campbell ducks are well known for their prodigious egg-laying skills, laying up to 300 eggs a year. Their khaki-colored feathers and slender body make them ideal for producing both meat and eggs.

Indian Runner ducks are distinguished by their energetic foraging habits and erect stance.

They are proficient egg layers and effective in managing pests in gardens and rice paddies, having originated from Indonesia. Other noteworthy breeds are the Mallard, Aylesbury, and Rouen, each of which has unique benefits based on the objectives of the farmer. Whether the breed is intended for meat, eggs, or pest management, selecting the appropriate one will maximize productivity and satisfy consumer demand.

ADVANTAGES OF RAISING DUCKS

Duck farming is a desirable agricultural endeavor due to its many advantages. The great productivity of ducks in terms of producing meat and eggs is one of the main benefits. Ducks develop quickly—they can reach market weight in a matter of weeks—and certain varieties are capable of producing large quantities of eggs each year. When compared to other cattle, this efficiency means faster returns on investment.

Ducks are robust and highly adaptive animals as well. They can flourish in a variety of habitats, including pastures, marshes, and even cities.

Their capacity to graze for a sizable amount of their food lowers feed costs and encourages environmentally friendly farming methods. Additionally, because ducks are less prone to common poultry diseases, fewer drugs are required, and overall management costs are decreased. Because of their hardiness, they may be raised in organic and free-range farms, which satisfies consumer desire for more sustainable and ethical products.

Duck farming also has positive environmental effects. By consuming weeds, snails, and insects, ducks help with natural pest control, which can increase crop yields and lessen the need for artificial pesticides. Their nutrient-rich excrement makes a fantastic natural fertilizer that raises soil health and productivity.

OBSTACLES IN DUCK FARMING

Duck farming has numerous advantages, but several difficulties must be overcome if farmers are to be successful. Managing water resources is one of the main issues.

For drinking, swimming, and preening, ducks need clean water, which can be hard to come by in places with little water sources. Pollution of the environment, unhygienic circumstances, and an increased risk of disease can all result from poor water management.

Another major problem in duck farming is predation. Predators including foxes, raccoons, and prey-seeking birds can harm ducks. Fencing and secure housing are necessary for flock protection, which can raise labor and expense prices. Furthermore, even though ducks are resilient animals, controlling parasites and infections is essential because they can still contract numerous illnesses. For flock health to be maintained and epidemics to be avoided, routine health monitoring, immunizations, and biosecurity measures are crucial.

Competition and changes in the market present further difficulties. Due to competition from other poultry sectors, cultural preferences, and economic conditions, there may be fluctuations in the market for duck products.

To reduce hazards, farmers must diversify their product lines and be up to date on market developments. A stable income and improved profitability can be achieved in the face of these difficulties by building a dependable client base and investigating niche markets, such as those for organic or specialty goods.

IMPORTANT WORDS AND DEFINITIONS

Anyone engaged in duck farming must be familiar with important terminology and definitions. "Brooding" is the term for taking care of young ducklings until they can control their body temperature and grow feathers. To promote healthy growth during this time, particular temperatures, humidity, and feeding conditions are needed. A "duck" is a female duck; a "drake" is a name used for a male duck. It's critical to understand the differences in managing flock composition and breed.

The technique known as "vent sexing" is used to ascertain the sex of ducklings, which is essential for maintaining production targets and breeding plans. This method looks for gender-specific traits in the duckling by looking at its vent area. "Molting" is the term for the yearly natural process by which ducks lose and grow back their feathers. Ducks may lay fewer eggs during molting and need more food to support the growth of new feathers.

The terms "pasture-raised" and "free-range" refer to farming practices where ducks are allowed access to outdoor spaces for exercise and foraging. These techniques are linked to better product quality and animal welfare. The term "biosecurity" describes procedures and safeguards put in place to stop the entry and spread of illnesses within a flock. This covers immunization schedules, cleanliness guidelines, and quarantine policies. Comprehending these terminologies facilitates farmers in executing efficient management strategies and optimizing their duck farming enterprises.

CHAPTER TWO

PUTTING YOUR DUCK FARM IN ORDER

CHOOSING AN APPROPRIATE LOCATION

Selecting an appropriate site for your duck farm is essential to its success. Choose a location where ducks can move around freely and exhibit their natural behaviors. Ducks require water to drink, bathe, and swim, so a place with access to clean water is necessary. To prevent contamination, make sure the location is clear of contaminants and far from industrial areas. Ducks can also be kept comfortable in an area with natural shade from trees or man-made buildings, which shields them from harsh weather.

Take the location's soil quality into consideration. Because ducks can be untidy, it's important to have adequate drainage to avoid water logging and preserve hygiene. Steer clear of low-lying locations that are prone to flooding since standing water might be unhealthy. To aid with drainage, the soil should be level or gradually sloping. Accessibility to a dependable power source is also necessary for the operation of machinery including lighting systems, feeds, and incubators. Being close to markets and roadways can make it easier to transfer goods and supplies, which will increase the effectiveness of your business.

Legal factors should be taken into account when choosing a place. To make sure you comply, check your local zoning laws and regulations surrounding animal production. Before you begin farming, be sure you have all the required licenses and permits.

Joining a farming community can also give you access to shared information and resources, as well as networking opportunities. All things considered, a carefully selected site will provide a solid basis for a successful and long-lasting duck farming business.

CREATING AND BUILDING DUCK HOUSES

To keep your ducks safe from disease, inclement weather, and predators, you must provide them with appropriate shelter. Provide enough room for each duck to walk around freely in their habitat; a minimum of 3–4 square feet should be allotted for each duck. Nesting, feeding, and resting areas should all be included in the home. Straw or wood shavings for bedding can offer comfort and insulation, while elevated floors with wire mesh can assist keep the space dry and clean.

An essential component of duck housing design is ventilation. Make sure some vents or windows let in fresh air to help prevent the accumulation of ammonia from duck droppings, which can be harmful to the respiratory systems of the birds. To endure the weather and possible wear and tear, the housing should be built using sturdy materials. Ducks should be shielded from rain and snow by waterproof roofing, and the building should be substantial enough to endure powerful gusts of wind.

A safe outside run should be constructed for the ducks in addition to the main house structure. Ducks can be shielded from ground and aerial predators by being kept in fenced cages with netting above. Access to a pond or other artificial water supply for swimming and foraging should be provided by the run. Adding vegetation, such as shrubs and grasses, can provide further protection and enrichment by simulating a natural habitat. Your duck flock's production and well-being will be guaranteed by well-designed and built housing.

ESSENTIAL INSTRUMENTS AND EQUIPMENT

Maintaining the health of your ducks and running your farm efficiently depend on having the correct tools and equipment. Start with duck-specific feeders and waterers to reduce waste and make sure they are conveniently accessible. Time and work can be saved using automatic feeders and waterers, especially for bigger flocks. To stop the transmission of illness, give these tools regular cleaning and disinfection.

If you intend to hatch ducklings on-site, use a dependable incubator. Hatching success rates can be raised by using contemporary incubators with temperature and humidity controls.

Ducklings need brooders equipped with heating plates or bulbs to stay warm in the early stages. To guarantee the health and development of the ducklings, keep an eye on the brooder environment and maintain a constant temperature. Keeping a first-aid kit filled with the equipment and drugs you need will also help you take care of any health problems right away.

Additional necessary tools include shovels, rakes, and wheelbarrows for waste and bedding management, as well as cleaning and maintenance gear. Enclosure construction and upkeep require fencing tools. Stock plenty of bedding items, such as wood shavings or straw, to keep the ducks' habitat tidy and cozy. You can optimize your farm's operations and provide your ducks with the best care possible by investing in high-quality gear and equipment.

GETTING WELL DUCKLINGS

Building a robust and fruitful flock requires starting your duck farm with healthy ducklings. Acquire ducklings from trustworthy hatcheries or breeders that are recognized for their superior and disease-free stock. Investigate possible suppliers and visit them to see their procedures and the environments in which the ducks are grown. Request certifications and medical documents to make sure the ducklings are immunized and free of common illnesses.

Look for energetic, aware ducklings with clear eyes, tidy noses, and silky, fluffy feathers when choosing your ducklings. Ducklings that seem listless, have discharge coming from their noses or eyes, or exhibit lameness should not be handled. To minimize stress and prevent injury or disease transmission, move the ducklings in a container with adequate ventilation. For a few weeks, quarantine newcomers to your flock to keep an eye on their health and stop them from bringing illnesses to others.

Build a strong rapport with your provider to receive assistance and guidance in the future. They can offer helpful advice on nutrition, health maintenance, and breeding techniques.

To preserve genetic diversity and increase the resilience of your brood, regularly obtain fresh ducklings. A strong and prosperous duck farming business is built on the foundation of healthy ducklings.

SETTING APART MONEY FOR STARTUP EXPENSES

Setting up money for initial expenses is an essential part of establishing your duck farm. Start by making a list of every possible expense, such as buying or leasing property, building homes, and buying tools and equipment. Take into account the price of bedding, feed, and ducklings. Donate money for immunizations, first vet care, and any prescription drugs that may be required. A thorough and reasonable assessment is essential to preventing unforeseen financial difficulties.

Your budget should account for operational expenses including labor, utilities, and maintenance. Preparing for these ongoing costs is crucial because they can quickly mount up. If you want to save money for unforeseen expenses like repairs or medical emergencies, think about creating a contingency fund. To obtain precise estimates, look up the costs of goods and services in your local market. Speaking with agricultural advisers or other duck farmers will help you improve your budget and gain valuable insights.

If you require funding, consider looking for agricultural loans, grants, or collaborations. New farmers might receive financial aid from several agricultural groups and government programs. Maintaining thorough financial documentation from the start will enable you to monitor costs and income, which will simplify any necessary budget adjustments. Budgeting effectively guarantees that you have the funds required to launch and maintain a profitable duck farming operation.

CHAPTER THREE

DIETARY AND FEEDING

THE NUTRITIOUS NEEDS OF DUCKS

For the sake of their well-being and productivity, ducks have particular dietary requirements that must be satisfied. A balance of protein, carbs, fats, vitamins, and minerals should be included in their diet. Ducks need a diet containing 16% to 18% protein for optimum growth and development.

This protein can be obtained from a variety of feed sources, including fish meal, soybean meal, and meat and bone meal. Grains like corn, wheat, and barley are great suppliers of carbohydrates, which are necessary for energy production. Fats, which come from things like vegetable oils, give birds the vital fatty acids they need to have good feathers and to be healthy generally.

For their bodies to function properly, ducks require vitamins and minerals in addition to macronutrients.

While vitamin D promotes calcium absorption for strong bones, vitamin A is essential for the immune system and visual health. As an antioxidant, vitamin E shields cells from harm. Minerals like phosphorus and calcium are essential for the development of eggshells and healthy bones. A good diet guarantees that ducks will develop healthily and yield high-quality meat or eggs.

FEED AND SUPPLEMENT TYPES

Depending on the ducks' age and purpose, different kinds of feed must be provided. Grower feeds offer balanced nutrition for development, whereas starter feeds are strong in protein to encourage growth in young ducklings.

For ducks in the egg-laying stage, layer meals are designed with extra calcium added for the strength of the eggshell. Probiotics and prebiotic supplements help maintain a healthy digestive system, and grit facilitates digestion by breaking down food in the gizzard.

Ducks that forage for food may eat insects, small fish, and aquatic plants, which will add natural nutrients to their diet. It's convenient to use pelleted meals to make sure ducks get all the nutrients they need in every bite. Ducks have specific dietary needs, and waterfowl diets are designed to satisfy those needs.

Higher niacin levels are necessary for healthy legs and high-quality feathers. Duck farmers can customize their feeding tactics for the best outcomes by having a thorough understanding of the various feed and supplement varieties.

FEEDING PLANS AND TIMETABLES

To keep ducks healthy and productive, a feeding program must be established. For fast growth, young ducks need to be fed four or six times a day on average. Adult ducks can cut back on feeding frequency to twice daily as they become older. It is essential to always have clean water available for ducks since they require it for digestion and to stay hydrated, particularly in hot weather or during egg-producing seasons.

Seasonal variations in dietary requirements, activity levels, and weather should all be taken into account when planning feeding schedules. It is possible to avoid underfeeding or overfeeding ducks by modifying feed amounts according to their behavior and body condition. You can determine whether adjustments are necessary by keeping an eye on feed consumption and studying duck behavior. In a farming setting, feeding schedules and routines that are consistent encourage ducks to eat healthily and to be generally well.

CONTROLLING THE QUALITY AND AVAILABILITY OF WATER

To guarantee that ducks have access to fresh, clean water for drinking and bathing, water management is essential in duck farming. Ducks submerge themselves in water on a natural inclination that helps them stay clean and regulates their body temperature. Waterborne illnesses and contamination are avoided by keeping shallow water sources easily accessible and cleaned regularly.

Testing for water quality is necessary to keep an eye on bacterial contamination, pH levels, and nutrient content, all of which are important for providing ducks with clean, safe water.

The best possible water quality is maintained with the use of filtration systems and routine upkeep of water sources. Enough room should be provided for ducks to get water without being crowded since this would lessen stress and encourage natural behaviors.

SPECIAL DIETARY REQUIREMENTS AND MODIFICATIONS

Ducks may require different diets according to their age, breed, level of health, and intended use for production. For instance, greater protein and calcium intake is necessary for breeding ducks throughout the mating and egg-producing phases. Higher protein levels help molting ducks regenerate their feathers. Veterinarians advised specialty meals or supplements may be necessary for ducks with health concerns.

Seasonal shifts and environmental stressors may also need dietary modifications. Supplements or feeds that have been fortified can assist treat certain dietary deficits or health issues. Throughout their lives, ducks are guaranteed the best possible nutrition and well-being by routine evaluation of their nutritional requirements and consultation with specialists in poultry nutrition.

CHAPTER FOUR

MANAGEMENT OF HEALTH AND DISEASE

TYPICAL DUCK ILLNESSES AND HOW TO PREVENT THEM

A key component of a profitable duck farming operation is knowing the prevalent diseases and how to avoid them. Several diseases, including Avian Influenza, Duck Viral Hepatitis, and Botulism, can affect ducks. For example, avian influenza can result in respiratory discomfort and reduced egg production. It is crucial to keep an environment clean and hygienic to prevent such disorders.

To lower the danger of respiratory illnesses, provide the duck housing area with regular cleaning and disinfection, supply clean water, and make sure there is enough ventilation.

Furthermore, a healthy diet is essential for preventing disease. Make sure ducks have access to a diet rich in key vitamins and minerals and well-balanced.

Don't give them tainted or rotten food. A veterinarian's routine health examinations are also essential for early disease identification and prevention. Customized vaccination regimens for your duck breed and area can improve overall flock health and disease resistance even more.

IMMUNIZATIONS AND HEALTH CARE

A vital component of duck husbandry is vaccination, which guards against frequent illnesses. To create a vaccination program that takes into account the unique requirements of your flock as well as the common diseases in your area, speak with a veterinarian. Vaccinations against diseases such as Newcastle disease and Duck Viral Hepatitis are necessary to keep the flock healthy. Vaccinate birds by advised protocols, and maintain thorough records of every bird's immunizations.

For a flock to remain healthy, routine medical care is equally important as vaccination. Keep a watchful eye out for any symptoms of disease in ducks, including decreased appetite, lethargic behavior, or unusual behavior. As soon as a duck becomes ill, separate it from the rest of the flock.

Administer any required medical care while working under a veterinarian's supervision. Frequent fecal and medical examinations can help identify and treat health problems early on, protecting your ducks' well-being.

IDENTIFYING SYMPTOMS OF ILLNESS

It's critical to identify early illness symptoms in ducks to act quickly to stop the spread of disease. Reduced activity, alterations in eating or drinking habits, respiratory distress, irregular feces, and abnormalities in feathers is common indicators of illness. Keep a regular eye out for any strange behavior or physical changes in your ducks.

As soon as sick ducks are noticed, separate them from other ducks to stop the disease from spreading. For an accurate diagnosis and recommended course of treatment, speak with a veterinarian.

Maintain thorough records of all symptoms seen and medications taken. Limit visitor access to the duck area and sanitize equipment as biosecurity measures to reduce the danger of illness transmission.

PROCEDURES FOR QUARANTINING NEW BIRDS

Careful quarantine protocols must be followed when adding new ducks to your flock to prevent the spread of disease. Quarantine new birds in a separate, isolated area away from existing flock members. During the two to four-week quarantine period, keep a sharp eye out for any symptoms of sickness.

Keep an eye out for any signs of respiratory distress, diarrhea, or unusual behavior in new birds throughout the quarantine period.

To find any underlying medical conditions, perform comprehensive health screenings, including fecal examinations. Avoid direct contact between confined birds and current flock members to prevent illness spread.

After the quarantine time, gradually introduce fresh birds to the existing flock while checking for any signs of sickness. Maintaining a healthy flock and stopping the spread of illnesses brought in by new birds depend on quarantine protocols.

TIPS FOR MAINTAINING A HEALTHY FLOCK

Careful attention to detail and proactive management are necessary to keep a duck flock in good health. Implement biosecurity measures, such as restricting visitor access, cleaning equipment, and maintaining proper hygiene, to reduce the risk of disease. Give ducks a well-balanced diet full of vital nutrients to help their immune system and general well-being.

Regularly clean and disinfect the duck housing area, water sources, and feeding equipment to reduce disease transmission. Every day, keep an eye on the behavior and health of the flock and record any changes or anomalies. Maintain thorough records of all the shots, examinations, and treatments given to your birds.

For immunization schedules, treatment plans, and preventive healthcare, see a veterinarian regularly.

A healthy and productive duck flock depends on early detection and intervention. Review and update health and biosecurity protocols regularly by industry standards and changing farm conditions.

CHAPTER FIVE

INCUBATION AND BREEDING

CHOOSING BREEDING STOCK

Selecting appropriate breeding stock is essential for a profitable duck farm. Begin by choosing genetically sound, healthy ducks. Seek for birds that are healthy, alert, and devoid of any abnormalities or diseases. Think about the breed features you want, including meat quality, egg production, or specific physical attributes. To make sure the ducks meet your breeding objectives, evaluate their conformation, size, and temperament.

Take into account the age of the ducks for breeding as well. Depending on the breed, ducks often attain sexual maturity between the ages of 4 and 7 months. Pick the best-suited ducks for breeding to optimize hatchability and fertility. For the best rates of mating and fertilization, it's also critical to keep the male-to-female breeding ratio balanced.

Finally, to avoid illness and maintain a healthy flock, regularly examine and vaccinate your breeding animals. Maintain thorough records of every duck's performance, including its ability to produce eggs, its fertility, and any health problems. You can use this knowledge to make well-informed judgments about future breeding choices and enhancements to your duck farming business.

BREEDING METHODS AND RECOMMENDED PRACTICES

In duck farming, artificial insemination and natural mating are the most often utilized breeding strategies. Ducks can couple up and marry spontaneously through a process called natural mating, but it also involves keeping the ideal male-to-female ratio and providing a breeding habitat.

Conversely, artificial insemination provides greater control over genetic variety and breeding results by requiring physical collection and insertion of semen into the female duck's reproductive canal.

Whichever approach you select, be sure that breeding season management procedures are followed. Give ducks enough food, fresh water, and a good place to live if you want to encourage mating behavior and reproductive health. Keep a watchful eye on reproductive rates and mating behavior to spot any problems early and take appropriate action.

To further enhance flock performance, think about introducing breeding programs that select desired features. Make educated breeding selections by utilizing pedigree analysis, genetic testing, and performance records. Continually assess and modify your breeding methods and strategies to maximize output and genetic variety within your duck flock.

EQUIPMENT AND THE INCUBATION PROCESS

Healthy ducklings need to hatch throughout the incubation period. Gather healthy, viable eggs from your breeding stock first. Until they are ready for incubation, store the eggs correctly in a cold, humidity-controlled environment.

For the best hatch rates, use high-quality egg incubators with accurate humidity and temperature settings.

Keep duck eggs at a constant temperature of about 99.5°F (37.5°C) and a humidity level of between 55 and 60% during incubation. To encourage healthy growth and stop the embryos from adhering to the shell membrane, turn the eggs frequently—at least three times a day. Track the weight loss of the eggs to verify that the incubator is properly ventilated and to modify the humidity levels as needed.

Reduce spinning and raise humidity levels as the hatching date draws near to aid in the hatching process. Give recently hatched duckling's access to a clean, warm brooder environment with food and water.

HANDLING DUCKLINGS AFTER HATCHING

Ducklings require appropriate care and management following hatching for them to grow and develop. Place the just hatched ducklings in a clean, well-ventilated brooder space with appropriate bedding.

Give duckling's access to fresh water and a beginning meal that has been specially designed to fulfill their dietary requirements.

Initially, keep the brooder temperature between 85 and 90°F (29 and 32°C), then progressively lower it as the ducklings develop feathers and become more tolerant to temperature fluctuations. Keep an eye out for any indications of disease, trauma, or stress in the ducklings, and if necessary, provide them with the proper veterinarian care.

By giving the brooder area enough room, enough ventilation, and frequent cleaning, you can encourage healthy growth.

Give ducklings enrichment activities to help them exercise and develop their natural habits, like as swimming in water. As they get older, gradually expose them to outdoor settings, making sure they are safe from predators and bad weather.

MAINTAINING DOCUMENTS FOR BREEDING PROGRAMS

In duck farming, successful breeding programs depend on accurate record-keeping. Maintain thorough records of your breeding stock, including statistics on performance, health, and pedigrees. Dates of breeding, results of mating, and number of eggs laid, rates of fertility, hatchability, and any illnesses or genetic abnormalities seen should all be noted.

Count the number of eggs, hatchlings, and adult ducks accurately to measure population increase and evaluate breeding success. To arrange and evaluate breeding data and spot patterns, program strengths, and areas for development, use software or handwritten records.

Review and adjust breeding objectives regularly in response to market demands and performance measures. To make well-informed choices on culling, breeding stock selection, and genetic advancements, consults historical data.

CHAPTER SIX

ENVIRONMENTAL MANAGEMENT AND HOUSING

CREATING COZY DUCK HOUSING

Ducks' health and welfare depend on the design of their cozy house. Determine how many ducks you want to maintain and how much room they'll need as your initial step. Ducks require lots of space to walk around, hunt, and get to water. Giving each duck at least 4 square feet of floor area is a standard thumb rule.

Next, think about the housing structure's design. Sufficient ventilation is necessary to guarantee the flow of fresh air and avoid respiratory problems. This can be accomplished by including windows or vents high up on the walls. Ducks are very sensitive to temperature changes, so the house needs to be insulated to keep the birds happy all year round.

Bedding and flooring are two other crucial components. Because ducks are dirty and excrete a lot, the flooring should be simple to keep clean. Straw and wood shavings are good bedding materials because they can absorb moisture and odor, keeping the ducks' habitat fresh and cozy.

CONTROLLING DENSITY AND SPACE

For the sake of the health and production of ducks, space and density management in housing is essential. Stress, the spread of disease, and decreased egg production can all result from overcrowding.

 Enough room must be allowed for every duck to be able to walk around freely, get food and water, and engage in their natural activities, such as preening and nesting.

Determine the right density by multiplying the number of ducks by the size of your housing building. By giving each duck the proper amount of space, you may prevent congestion. Enough space also discourages aggressive behavior and encourages a peaceful, well-groomed flock.

Observe the flock's behavior regularly and modify the space as necessary. If the ducks are showing symptoms of stress or overpopulation, think about lowering the number of ducks in the flock or increasing their living space. Effective space management has a major impact on the general health and welfare of flocks.

CONTROLLING TEMPERATURE AND VENTILATION

Controlling temperature and ventilation are essential components of managing duck housing. In addition to removing excess moisture and ammonia from droppings and ensuring fresh air circulation, proper ventilation also guards against respiratory problems.

Provide housing structures with windows, vents, or fans to let air circulate without putting the ducks in danger of drafts.

Keep the housing's temperature at ideal levels. Because they are sensitive to temperature changes, make sure the housing is adequately insulated to maintain a comfortable temperature in both hot and cold climates.

To avoid heat stress, use heaters or heat lamps in the winter and offer shade or other cooling options in the summer.

Check the housing's interior temperature and humidity levels regularly. Install hygrometers and thermometers to monitor the environment and make any modifications. A habitat that is both comfortable and healthy for ducks is facilitated by appropriate ventilation and temperature regulation.

BEDDING AND HANDLING OF LITTER

To keep duck housing hygienic and tidy, efficient bedding and litter control are crucial. Select bedding materials that efficiently absorb moisture and odor, such as wood shavings, shredded paper, or straw. To give the ducks comfort and insulation, cover the floor with a thick layer of bedding.

Maintain regular bedding cleaning and replacement to avoid ammonia and bacterial accumulation. Ducks generate a lot of waste, so keeping the area clean and healthy requires regular cleaning. Clean bedding should be removed using a shovel or rake and replaced with new stuff.

Regularly check the bedding's condition. If it gets wet or dirty easily, change the bedding's thickness or cleaning schedule appropriately. Well-maintained bedding minimizes odors, enhances health, and gives ducks a cozy place to rest.

STRATEGIES TO PROTECT AGAINST PREDATORS

Putting into practice practical predator-reduction tactics is essential to guaranteeing ducks' security and safety. Determine which animals, such as foxes, raccoons, and prey-seeking birds, could be present in your area and secure the dwelling structure appropriately. Use fences that are robust and have buried wire mesh to keep ground predators from digging and getting inside.

To stop unwanted entrances, install locks on windows and doors that are predator-proof. To ward against nocturnal predators, think about installing motion-activated lights or sirens. Make quick repairs after routinely checking the perimeter for indications of damage or attempted intrusions.

Give ducks safe places to spend the night, including enclosed shelters or enclosures that are impenetrable by predators. Place predator guards on coop entrances to keep predators from accessing the area, and raise nesting boxes to discourage ground-based predators. By putting these tactics into practice, the danger of predation is decreased and ducks are given a safe environment.

CHAPTER SEVEN

EVERYDAY HANDLING AND ADMINISTRATION

TYPICAL MAINTENANCE AND CARE

A systematic approach is essential for routine care and maintenance in duck farming to maximize productivity and ensure the welfare of your flock.

Start by creating a daily schedule that includes chores like assessing the quantity and quality of the water, examining the feed, and keeping an eye on the ducks' general health. Maintaining a clean and hygienic atmosphere and preventing waste buildup need routine cleaning of the duck housing area. As needed, this includes cleaning the bedding, feeders, and waterers.

Additionally, keep an eye on your ducks' health by doing routine examinations. This entails keeping an eye on their behavior, looking for any indications of disease or damage, and dealing with any problems as soon as they appear.

Incorporating vaccinations and parasite management into your regular healthcare regimen is essential for disease prevention and preserving your flock's health. Make sure ducks have access to a varied meal that satisfies their needs at all growth stages because proper nutrition is equally important.

Maintaining infrastructure and equipment used in duck farming, including gates, fences, and ventilation systems, should be done regularly. Maintaining these items properly not only increases their longevity but also guarantees your ducks' comfort and safety. You may produce an environment that is favorable to the health and productivity of duck farming by creating a thorough routine for care and maintenance.

HOW TO MOVE AND HANDLE DUCKS SAFELY

A vital component of duck farming is the proper handling and transportation of the birds, which calls for close attention to reduce stress and potential harm to the birds. When working with ducks take a calm attitude and don't make abrupt moves that could frighten them.

When lifting and carrying ducks, use gentle handling techniques and provide appropriate body support to prevent discomfort or injury. To prevent needless tension, it's critical to pay attention to the ducks' behavior and adjust your response appropriately.

Use suitable crates or containers that offer enough room and ventilation while transferring or moving ducks between locations. Make sure there are no sharp edges or protrusions in the containers that could hurt the ducks while they are being transported.

Duck movements should be coordinated during the cooler parts of the day to minimize heat stress, particularly in hot weather.

Keep a vigilant eye out for any indications of suffering or injury in the ducks as they are being handled and moved. Be ready to handle any problems that come up during the process or to give emergency care. You may protect your ducks' welfare and reduce the hazards involved in handling and transferring them by adhering to safe handling procedures and using caution when transporting them.

TRACKING THE HEALTH AND BEHAVIOR OF DUCKS

It takes constant observation, familiarity with typical duck habits and sickness indicators, and understanding of duck behavior and health to monitor duck behavior and health. Keeps a close eye on your ducks' behavior, observing their general temperament, social interactions, feeding habits, and activity levels. Behavior changes, like reduced activity, sluggishness, or hostility, may point to underlying medical conditions that need to be addressed.

Aside from behavior monitoring, make sure your ducks are healthy regularly. This entails assessing their overall health, looking for indications of parasites or wounds, and keeping an eye on their water and food intake. Any anomalies or worries should be taken care of right away by speaking with a veterinarian or starting the proper course of action.

Maintain thorough notes of your observations and health evaluations to monitor trends, spot patterns, and spot any reoccurring problems. With this knowledge, you may optimize your duck flock's health and well-being by making well-informed decisions about nutritional changes, healthcare interventions, and management techniques. Successful duck farming requires proactive management of the health and behavior of the birds as well as routine observation.

ADJUSTMENTS FOR SEASONAL CARE

To adapt to shifting climatic conditions and maintain the comfort and health of your flock all year round, seasonal care modifications are essential in the duck farming industry. To keep ducks from being overheated during hot weather, make sure they have access to cold, clean water and plenty of shade. To assist control temperature and humidity levels in living rooms, think about adding fans or misting systems.

Make sure ducks have enough shelter from wind, dampness, and cold throughout the winter months.

Give ducks bedding or insulated shelters to keep them dry and comfortable. To meet the dietary needs of ducks during colder months, modify feeding schedules to take into consideration variations in energy requirements and provide nutrient-dense feeds.

In addition, seasonal care entails modifying management techniques—like breeding plans, egg collection frequency, and predator control tactics—in response to seasonal patterns and obstacles.

Assess the state of the equipment, water supplies, and dwelling structures regularly to make sure it is functioning at their best and to handle any seasonal maintenance requirements.

You can encourage the health and productivity of your duck flock all year round by modifying management techniques to account for environmental factors and seasonal changes.

EFFECTIVE TECHNIQUES FOR FARM MANAGEMENT

To ensure sustainable operations in duck farming and to maximize productivity while minimizing expenses, effective farm management strategies are crucial. For your duck farming enterprise, start by clearly defining your goals and objectives. These should include production targets, budgetary targets, and sustainability goals. Create a thorough farm management plan that details how to accomplish these objectives while maximizing resources and reducing waste.

Use premium feeds that are formulated to meet the specific nutritional requirements of ducks at various phases of their lives to implement effective feeding methods. To maximize growth rates and feed conversion ratios, keep an eye on feed consumption and make necessary adjustments to feeding schedules or formulations. Effective waste management techniques can lessen their negative effects on the environment and create new sources of income, such as composting manure or using it as fertilizer.

To increase productivity and streamline farm operations, make use of automation and technology. This comprises computerized record-keeping systems for managing inventory, medical information, and financial transactions; data monitoring tools for tracking performance metrics; and automated feeding systems. Review and evaluate farm performance data regularly to pinpoint areas that need work and put focused optimization tactics into action.

To keep up to current on industry best practices, new technologies, and regulatory needs, invest in continual education and training for yourself and your farm workers. To stay competitive and succeed in duck farming over the long run, it's important to regularly assess and modify farm management techniques in response to input, performance information, and shifting market conditions.

CHAPTER EIGHT

SALES AND MARKETING

FINDING OPPORTUNITIES IN THE MARKET

Finding market potential is the first step in entering the world of duck farming. Start by looking at regional and international duck industry trends. Examine elements such as consumer inclinations, the market for duck eggs and meat, and new markets. To learn more about the requirements and preferences of potential clients, conduct surveys or interviews with them.

Analyze your competitors after that. Locate additional local duck farms or websites that sell duck items. Examine their clientele, pricing policies, and areas of strength and weakness. You can take advantage of unexplored chances and uniquely establish your duck farming business with the aid of this information.

Finally, think about diversity. Look into possible markets that need duck products but are underserved.

For example, there may be potential in niche markets such as those for organic duck meat or unusual duck items. You may build a solid basis for the success of your duck farming endeavor by recognizing and seizing market possibilities.

FORMULATING A MARKETING STRATEGY AND BRAND

The next stage after determining market prospects for your duck farming business is to develop a strong brand and marketing strategy. Establish your brand identity at the outset by outlining your values, mission, and USPs. Create a memorable and appealing brand name, logo, and tagline that appeals to your intended market.

Create a thorough marketing plan after that. Choose the market sectors you want to target, such as direct consumers, restaurants, and supermarkets. Create approaches to connect with each target audience, such as social media campaigns, digital marketing, partnerships with nearby companies, and attendance at food festivals or farmers' markets.

Think about how storytelling can help your marketing campaigns. Talk about your experience as a duck farmer, emphasize the sustainable methods you use on your property, and highlight the high caliber and freshness of your duck goods. To draw in and keep customers, use product photos, client testimonials, and interesting material.

You may successfully advertise your duck farming company and draw in a devoted clientele by developing a strong brand presence and carrying out a carefully considered marketing strategy.

PRICING METHODS FOR PRODUCTS AND DUCKS

Pricing your ducks and duck-related goods correctly is essential to your business's success and capacity to compete. To start, do a cost study to ascertain the costs associated with duck farming, such as labor, housing, feed, and overhead. To determine the starting pricing for your products, take the intended profit margin into account.

Next, think about pricing schemes like cost-plus pricing, in which a markup is added to cover expenses and make a profit. Value-based pricing is another option you may consider, where prices are determined by how much buyers think your things are worth. To position your items competitively and gain insight into competitors' pricing strategies, conduct market research.

Don't discount seasonal promotions, discounts for large orders, or product bundling as ways to increase sales. To stay competitive and increase revenue in the ever-changing duck farming industry, keep an eye on market trends and modify your pricing methods accordingly.

TRADER OF DUCKS AND DUCK PRODUCTS

Now that your pricing and marketing tactics are set, you can concentrate on efficiently selling your ducks and duck-related products. To reach a larger audience, think about utilizing a variety of sales channels, such as your farm's direct sales, internet platforms, neighborhood markets, eateries, and specialized shops.

Make an investment in eye-catching labeling and packaging that represents your business. To improve client experience and happiness, emphasize the main features of the product, its nutritional facts, and its cooking instructions. To gain the trust of customers, make sure that food safety laws and certifications are followed.

To generate discussion about your items, use sales promotions like first-time incentives, loyalty plans, or partnerships with chefs or influencers. Deliver exceptional customer service and ensure follow-up to encourage recurring business and great word-of-mouth referrals.

You may increase sales and establish a stronger position in the cutthroat duck farming industry by broadening your sales channels, refining the way your products are presented, and providing outstanding customer service.

DEVELOPING RELATIONSHIPS WITH CUSTOMERS

Developing enduring and solid client relationships is crucial to your duck farming business's long-term success. Through surveys, reviews, and interactions, get a basic grasp of your consumers' preferences, comments, and purchasing behavior. Make efficient use of this information to customize your offerings to suit their demands.

Be open and honest with your customers about your agricultural methods, the caliber of your products, and any pertinent updates or special offers. Use social media, newsletters, and events to interact with them and win their trust and loyalty. To demonstrate your dedication to client happiness, invite testimonials and feedback from satisfied customers.

Use client retention techniques to encourage recurring business and word-of-mouth recommendations, such as personalized offers, birthday discounts, or referral schemes. To preserve your brand's good name and consumer confidence, respond to any problems or grievances from customers in a timely and professional manner.

A devoted customer base that promotes the expansion and sustainability of your duck farming business may be built by placing a high priority on building connections with customers, paying attention to their opinions, and providing outstanding value.

CHAPTER NINE

MONEY HANDLING

FINANCIAL PLANNING AND BUDGETING

Financial planning and budgeting are essential to the success of any duck farming enterprise. Start by listing every expense related to establishing and maintaining your duck farm. This covers the price of housing, food, vet care, equipment, and advertising. To establish a reasonable budget, check the market rates for ducklings, feed, and other necessities. Set up money for unforeseen costs and emergencies to prevent future financial hardship.

The process of financial planning entails projecting income and expenses for a given time frame, usually a year. To predict when money will come in and when bills are due, create a cash flow projection. This aids in efficiently managing cash flow and guarantees that you always have adequate money to pay for expenses. To maximize profitability, take into account seasonal variations in the market for meat or duck eggs and modify your financial plan appropriately.

By putting in place a system for financial planning and budgeting, you can monitor your progress and make wise choices.

Review your financial plan and budget regularly to find areas for improvement and make any necessary strategy adjustments. In the duck farming business, you can overcome obstacles and seize chances if you have a carefully considered financial plan.

STRATEGIES FOR COST MANAGEMENT AND REDUCTION

To keep duck farming profitable, cost control is crucial. Find places where expenses can be cut without sacrificing output or quality first. This could entail haggling over more affordable supplier costs, improving feed formulations for maximum financial return, and putting effective energy-saving techniques into place on farms.

Leverage technology and contemporary farming methods to optimize workflows and save labor expenses. Automated feeding systems, for instance, can reduce waste and labor hours, while equipment placement and farm architecture can maximize workflow efficiency. Evaluate operating expenditures regularly and look for creative ways to save costs without sacrificing the quality of care you provide for your ducks.

Continuous monitoring and evaluation are necessary when implementing cost-reduction initiatives. Examine financial records regularly and examine cost trends to find places where additional savings might be made. You may raise profitability and strengthen the overall financial stability of your duck farming business by taking proactive cost management measures.

MAINTAINING DOCUMENTS AND FINANCIAL MONITORING

In duck farming, maintaining accurate records is essential for monitoring finances and making decisions.

Keep thorough records of your earnings, outlays, inventory, and production indicators. To create precise reports for analysis and methodically arrange financial data, use spreadsheets or accounting software.

Monitor critical performance metrics like sales volumes, mortality rates, feed conversion ratios, and egg production. This information gives you important insights into the well-being and financial success of your duck farming business. Make educated company decisions by routinely updating records and analyzing trends to pinpoint areas that want improvement.

Monitoring cash flow, debt levels, and profitability ratios are other aspects of financial tracking. To evaluate the financial standing of your duck farm, use financial statements including cash flow, income, and balance sheets. Maintaining accurate and timely records helps you to identify patterns in your finances, take quick action when necessary, and take advantage of expansion opportunities.

INVESTMENT AND FINANCING OPTIONS

Establishing and growing a profitable duck farming enterprise requires obtaining sufficient capital. Investigate your possibilities for funding, including savings on your own, bank loans, grants from the government, and investor partnerships. Consider the benefits and drawbacks of each choice in light of the interest rates, terms of repayment, and possible effects on the financial stability of your company.

To determine your funding requirements and create a strategic financing plan, think about consulting with agricultural specialists or financial consultants. To entice possible lenders or investors, draft a thorough business plan that details the objectives, projected costs, and anticipated returns on investment of your duck farming enterprise.

Investing in duck farming might involve a variety of strategies, such as modernizing facilities, increasing output, introducing technological advancements, or diversifying product lines.

ANALYSIS AND STRATEGIES OF PROFITABILITY

To maximize profits and maintain a successful duck farming operation, profitability analysis is crucial. Determine important financial parameters including breakeven point, ROI, net profit margin, and gross profit margin. To evaluate the financial performance of your farm, compare these measures with historical data and industry comparisons.

Determine the variables that affect profitability, including the cost of production, market prices, changes in demand, and operational effectiveness. Implement tactics to boost profitability, such as enhancing feed conversion rates, reducing input costs, diversifying revenue streams, and optimizing marketing strategies to maximize sales.

Regularly examine and change pricing strategy depending on market dynamics and competitive data. To fulfill demand, prevent overstocking or underutilization of resources, and track and modify production levels.

CHAPTER TEN

FAQS & FREQUENTLY ASKED QUESTIONS

TAKING CARE OF COMMON ISSUES IN DUCK FARMING

Knowing what kind of accommodation ducks need is a common question among new duck farmers. Ducks require a haven to keep them safe from predators and inclement weather. A good duck home should provide the birds plenty of room to walk around and have enough ventilation to keep them from getting respiratory problems. It is imperative to utilize bedding items that will absorb moisture and keep the ducks dry, such as wood shavings or straws.

Sufficient feeding of ducks for their growth and well-being is another issue. A balanced diet of grains, greens, and sources of protein such as commercial duck feed or insects are necessary for ducks. Ducks require clean water for washing and drinking since it helps with digestion and maintains the health of their feathers. For optimum health, it is crucial to keep an eye on their food intake and modify their diet based on their developmental stage.

For duck farmers, controlling duck health and preventing illnesses is also very important. Maintaining a healthy flock depends on routine medical examinations, immunizations, and good hygiene. Disease outbreaks can be avoided by maintaining a clean habitat for the ducks, giving them regular access to fresh water, and keeping an eye out for any anomalies or symptoms of illness. It is advised that novice duck farmers seek advice from a veterinarian regarding treatment choices and preventive care.

COMMONLY ASKED QUESTIONS

Questions on duck breeds appropriate for their farming objectives are frequently asked by novice duck farmers. Farmers can select duck breeds that are best for producing eggs, producing meat, or having multiple purposes by having a thorough understanding of the traits and uses of each breed. Well-known duck breeds with a reputation for laying eggs and adapting to different farming conditions include Pekin, Khaki Campbell, and Indian Runner.

The process of duck egg incubation and hatching is another frequently asked question. Duck eggs normally take 28 days to hatch, and a successful hatch depends on the incubator's temperature and humidity levels being kept at the right levels.

Hatch rates can be increased by periodically rotating eggs during incubation and candling eggs to monitor embryo growth. After hatching, ducklings must have access to a safe, warm place to brood. This is crucial for their survival.

To safeguard their flock, duck farmers also ask about predator control strategies. Predators like foxes, raccoons, and birds of prey can be discouraged by erecting sturdy fencing, utilizing deterrents like motion-activated lighting or sound systems, and maintaining the cleanliness of the duck house and its surroundings.

Farmers can take prompt action to protect their ducks by putting in place routine patrols and keeping an eye out for indications of predator activity on the property.

TROUBLESHOOTING TYPICAL ISSUES

Dealing with problems related to water quality in ponds or other water sources is a typical challenge in duck husbandry. Ducks' health issues can be caused by poor water quality, which can also have an impact on their growth and egg production.

It is crucial to test water regularly for bacterial contamination, ammonia levels, and pH. Ducks can have the best possible water quality maintained by installing filtration systems, and aerators, and routinely cleaning water sources.

Controlling aggressive behavior and flock behavior is another problem, particularly during breeding seasons. Aggressive behavior among ducks can result in injuries and stress for the flock as a whole. Having adequate room, acclimating new ducks gradually, and keeping aggressive ducks apart can all assist in lessening conflict. Another way to reduce aggressive behavior is to create stimulating habitats with lots of foraging opportunities and distractions.

For duck farmers, managing pests and parasites is another frequent concern. External parasites that can impact duck health and egg production include lice and mites. Controlling infestations can be achieved by regularly implementing parasite preventive methods, including as cleaning and disinfecting housing places, utilizing bedding materials resistant to pests, and administering the proper treatments to ducks. For effective control, speaking with a veterinarian about parasite management techniques is advised.

SOURCES FOR ADDITIONAL EDUCATION

A variety of materials are available to assist novice duck farmers in their quest for deeper understanding and direction. Online communities and forums devoted to chicken farming provide insightful commentary, guidance, and encouragement from knowledgeable and seasoned farmers. Gaining knowledge and expertise in topics like disease control, breeding, and duck care can be accomplished by taking part in training courses, webinars, or workshops centered on duck farming.

Duck farming-specific instructional resources, including books, manuals, and online courses, can offer thorough guidance on best practices, common problem-solving techniques, and maximizing farm output.

Accessing government agricultural extension services or speaking with local poultry associations can also give significant resources, research findings, and regulatory information pertinent to duck farming operations.

Interacting with research centers, universities, and industry experts in agriculture can provide access to scientific studies, case studies, and cutting-edge technology related to duck farming. Engaging in agricultural shows and field days, visiting prosperous duck farms, and forming connections with other farmers can offer valuable perspectives, motivation, and networking prospects for ongoing education and enhancement of duck farming techniques.

SUGGESTIONS FOR PROLONGED ACHIEVEMENT

Proactive management techniques, ongoing learning, and thorough planning are necessary for duck farming to succeed in the long run. Creating a thorough farm management plan with objectives, approaches, and deadlines can assist monitor progress and offer a successful road map. Purchasing high-quality supplies, machinery, and infrastructure that are appropriate for duck farming operations can increase productivity and efficiency on the farm.

By putting into practice sustainable farming techniques including producing organic feed, conserving water, and managing trash, farms can improve their long-term viability and environmental stewardship. To maximize farm performance and pinpoint areas for improvement, important performance metrics like disease incidence, feed conversion ratios, and egg production rates should be routinely monitored.

Developing trusting bonds with vendors, clients, and industry players can open doors for cooperation, market expansion, and company development. Making educated decisions and adjusting to changing market conditions can be facilitated by keeping up to date on customer preferences, market trends, and regulatory changes about the poultry sector. A successful and long-lasting duck farming business can benefit from ongoing training and development for farm staff, including courses on skill development, animal care procedures, and safety regulations.

www.ingramcontent.com/pod-product-compliance
Lightning Source LLC
Chambersburg PA
CBHW071840210526
45479CB00001B/215